Contents

A Laugh a Day 2
Daft Definitions 3
Proverbial Pandemonium 4
Goofy Games 7
   Lighthouse 7
   Around the World 10
Crack the Code 12
Super-Secret Messages 14
Going Nuts 16
Joke Cookies 18
Just Kidding 20
A Silly Story 22
Mad Mix-Ups 23

A Laugh a Day

Q: How do you stop a fish from smelling?
A: Hold its nose!

There is no doubt about it, we all enjoy a good joke. There are many different types of humour, from simple puns to elaborate riddles.

A pun is a joke that plays with the meaning of words:

Q: Why did the man take a pencil to bed?
A: To draw the curtains.

A riddle is a puzzling question:

Q: What is as light as air but cannot be held for long?
A: Your breath.

Whether you prefer jokes, fun games, or silly stories, a laugh a day keeps the doctor away!

Daft Definitions

- Someone whose career is in ruins –   archaeologist
- What toads sit on when they're tired –   toadstools
- The building with the most stories –   library
- What you can always count on when things go wrong –   fingers
- A line of people waiting to have their hair cut –   barbecue
- A dance for a lot of small cakes – abundance

Proverbial Pandemonium

Shouting Proverbs
This is a fun game to play with your class, and teachers will tell you that it's a good listening game.

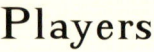

Players
Six to twenty people can play. With a larger group of people, you might want to have several "victims".

You Will Need
A list of proverbs. (A proverb is a very old and wise saying.) Here are some proverbs to help you get started:

- Too many cooks spoil the broth.
- Many hands make light work.
- A stitch in time saves nine.
- Haste makes waste.
- A bird in the hand is worth two in the bush.
- A watched pot never boils.
- An apple a day keeps the doctor away.
- Don't judge a book by its cover.
- Look before you leap.
- Don't count your chickens before they hatch.
- People who live in glass houses shouldn't throw stones.

How to Play

- One person is sent out of the room. The others choose a proverb. The words of the proverb are divided up so that each person has one word. If there aren't enough words, several people can have the same one.
- The "victim" is brought back and asks, "Tell me! Tell me! Tell me, do! What is the proverb that's special for you?"
- Everyone shouts at once, calling out their word. The listener tries to guess the proverb.
- If the victim doesn't guess it, then he or she has one more chance to ask, "Tell me! Tell me! Tell me, do..." Two points are awarded for guessing correctly the first time, one point if it takes two attempts, and no points for having to be told the answer.

Variations
Instead of proverbs, try using the titles of books, movies, or TV shows.

Goofy Games

Lighthouse

This game is fun, but it pays to move anything breakable out of the way before you start!

Players

Eight to twenty people can play.

You Will Need

Blindfolds for half the group and lots of floor space.

How to Play

- Divide into two teams: one team is the ships, and the other is the harbour.
- The ships are sent out of the room while the harbour gets organized.
- The harbour team needs to use the whole room. Some people will be "sandbars" and lie

on the ground, making the "sshussh!" sound of water flowing over sand. Some will crouch down as "rocks" and make the sound of waves crashing against them. Others will be "lighthouses" and make foghorn sounds to warn of dangerous reefs. One person will be the "wharf", where the ships have to tie up. The wharf should make a quiet, "Beep, beep! Beep, beep!" noise.

- One person is the "harbour pilot". When the harbour is ready, the pilot is sent out to bring the blindfolded "ships" to the harbour entrance.

- The harbour comes to life with the sounds of waves breaking on dangerous rocks and sandbars, etc. In the distance is the place the ships have to reach – the wharf. The ships set sail through the treacherous waters. If they touch anyone, they must immediately sink to the bottom of the harbour and remain there in silence until the game is over. No "ship" is safe until it has docked at the wharf.
- The game is over when all the ships have either reached the wharf or sunk. The teams then trade roles.

Around the World

Players
Three to thirty people can play.

You Will Need
An atlas or a world map.

How to Play
- Everyone sits in a circle.
- Player 1 begins. Here's an example of how to play:

Player 1: Annabelle, I hear you went on a holiday to Belgium.
Annabelle: Yes, I did.
Player 1: And what did you see in Belgium?
Annabelle: I saw big baskets of buns!

Annabelle turns to someone else.
Annabelle: Terry, I hear you went on a holiday to Copenhagen.
Terry: Yes, I did.

Annabelle: And what did you see in Copenhagen?
Terry: I saw crates of crazy crocodiles!

Do you get it? The first person thinks of a country, or any place name, and then asks someone to say what they saw there. The reply must include three words that start with the same first letter of the place, for example, for Belgium, it could be "big", "baskets", and "buns"; and for Copenhagen, it could be "crates", "crazy", and "crocodiles". If you're very clever, you may be able to think of more than three words!

Crack the Code

Have you ever wished you could send messages to a friend that no one else could read? Well, now you can!

Can you read the joke that is hidden in this set of numbers?

34: 46-16-2-40   16-2-38   2
26-30-42-40-16   4-42-40
6-2-28-28-30-40   40-2-24-22?
2: 2   36-18-44-10-36

This is a very easy code. (That is, when you know the secret!)

Every time you want to write the letter A, you write 2.

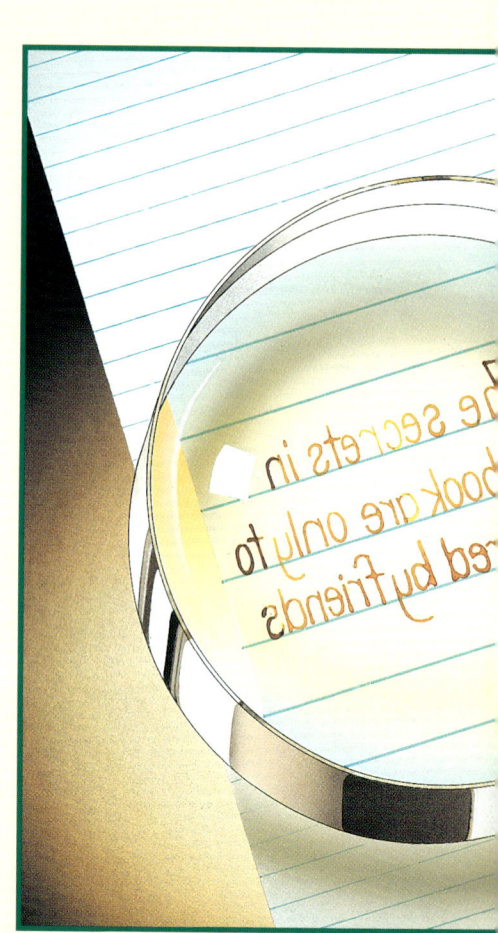

Every time you want to write the letter B, you write 4. For the letter C, you write 6. And so on...

| A is 2 | B is 4 | C is 6 | D is 8 | E is 10 | F is 12 | G is 14 | H is 16 | I is 18 | J is 20 | K is 22 | L is 24 | M is 26 | N is 28 | O is 30 | P is 32 | Q is 34 | R is 36 | S is 38 | T is 40 | U is 42 | V is 44 | W is 46 | X is 48 | Y is 50 | Z is 52 |

Now that you've cracked the code, you can find the hidden joke.

Show this secret joke to your friends, and ask them, "Can you read this joke?"

If they can't read it, show them how the code works. Soon you'll be able to send secret messages and jokes to each other.

Super-Secret Messages

If you want to make your secret message so secret that no one even knows you have written it, you can be really sneaky and write with invisible ink.

This is very easy to do, although you may have to experiment before you get it to work properly. The ingredients you need are all things you can find around your house.

Lemon juice, onion juice, and milk all make very good invisible inks.

Lemon Juice

Lemon-juice ink is made by squeezing the juice of half a lemon into a saucer. Dip a toothpick into the juice, then use it to write your message on white paper. It is best to use paper with lines, otherwise you cannot see where you are writing. To make your ink visible, *heat the paper. Iron your paper with an iron set on its lowest heat, or hold the paper close to an electric light that has been turned on for a while. The ink will show up so you can read the message.

Onion Juice

Onion-juice ink is used the same way as lemon-juice ink. It is hard to squeeze juice from an onion, so grate a small onion over a saucer, and soon you will find you have enough juice to write your message. *Heat your paper to read your message.

Milk

Milk will write in the same way. Again, you must *heat your paper to read the message.

*DO NOT HEAT YOUR PAPER OVER A FIRE OR A CANDLE.

Going Nuts
(makes 20 balls)

You Will Need
½ cup chocolate hail
1 cup chopped nuts
2 tablespoons icing sugar
6 tablespoons sweetened condensed milk
3 tablespoons chocolate chips
3 tablespoons crunchy peanut butter

Method
1. Place a sheet of waxed paper on a tray.

2. Pour the chocolate hail into a small bowl. Put half of the cup of chopped nuts into another small bowl.

3. Put the icing sugar, condensed milk, chocolate chips, peanut butter, and the rest of

the chopped nuts into a bowl. Mix well with a wooden spoon.

4. Take small teaspoonfuls of the mixture and roll into balls in the palms of your hands.

5. Roll the balls in the chocolate hail or chopped nuts until they are coated.

6. Place the balls on the prepared tray and refrigerate for 30 minutes.

Use brightly coloured giftwrap to cover a yoghurt container or a paper cup. Glue ribbon in place for a handle.

Cut coloured foil to make a frill and add this to make a festive band at the top.

Joke Cookies
(makes about 30 cookies)

Here's a way to get a joke across – deliciously! On small pieces of paper, write some jokes. Then hide the jokes in these home-made cookies for family and friends to find.

You Will Need
3 egg whites
1 teaspoon vanilla essence
¾ cup sugar
½ cup butter or margarine, melted
⅛ teaspoon salt
2 tablespoons water
1 cup flour

Method
1. Beat the egg whites, sugar, and salt together in a bowl. Add flour, vanilla, butter, and water, stirring well after each ingredient.

2. Chill the batter one hour in the refrigerator.

3. Write your jokes on small pieces of paper. Fold the papers. (You will need about 30 jokes.)

4. Drop the batter onto a greased cookie tray, one teaspoonful at a time. Spread each spoonful into a 10-cm circle with the back of a spoon (the batter must be very thin). Bake only three or four cookies at a time (they must be folded while they are still warm).

5. Bake the cookies at 175°C (350°F) for about 5 minutes, or until the edges start to brown. Carefully remove the cookies from the cookie tray and place them upside down on a clean surface. Let them cool for a few seconds, then place a message in the centre of each cookie. Fold the cookie in half, and then in quarters, and let it cool completely.

Just Kidding

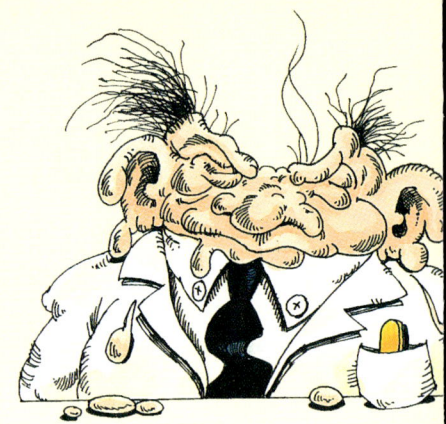

Q: What happened to the plastic surgeon who sat too close to the fire?
A: He melted.

Q: Which vitamin gives you good eyesight?
A: Vitamin C.

Q: How many ears did Davy Crockett have?
A: Three – a right ear, a left ear, and a wild frontier.

Q: What do you get when you cross a funny bone and a hand?
A: A humorist.

Q: Where did Sir Lancelot learn to be so brave?
A: At knight school.

Q: How did the Vikings send their secret messages?
A: By Norse code.

A Silly Story

Three men were lost on a freezing mountain. They sat down to make some tea. One man rubbed his hands on the kettle to make himself warm. Out jumped a genie, who offered them three wishes.

The first man wished he was back with his family. In a flash, he was back home.

The second man wished he was back home as well, and he, too, disappeared.

"I'm feeling very lonely," said the last man. "I wish my friends were back with me."

Mad Mix-Ups

Can you match the words on the right with their daft definitions on the left?

1. What the weather reporter would do with a ladder
2. A rough noise made by a tree
3. A cure for tired criminals
4. What the aircraft pilot said as she baled out
5. The part of a fish that weighs the most
6. A large, sick bird

Scales
Climate
Biplane
Arrest
Illegal
Bark

Answers: 1. Climate 2. Bark 3. Arrest 4. Biplane 5. Scales 6. Illegal

WHEN THINGS GO WRONG
The Long Walk Home
The Trouble with Patrick
The Kids from Quiller's Bend
Laughter is the Best Medicine
Wild Horses
The Sunday Horse

ANOTHER TIME, ANOTHER PLACE
Cloudcatcher
Flags
The Dinosaur Connection
Myth or Mystery?
Where Did the Maya Go?
The Journal: Dear Future II

SOMETHING STRANGE
My Father the Mad Professor
A Theft in Time: Timedetectors II
CD and the Giant Cat
Chocolate!
White Elephants and Yellow Jackets
Dream Boat

CONFIDENCE AND COURAGE
Imagine This, James Robert
Follow That Spy!
Who Will Look Out for Danny?
Fuzz and the Glass Eye
Bald Eagles
Cottle Street

Our thanks to the following authors for their contribution: **Ron Bacon** (pp. 12-15; pp. 18-19); **Paul Robinson** (pp. 20-21); **Alan Trussell-Cullen** (pp. 4-11).
Illustrated by **Madeline Beasley** (pp. 14-15); **Kelvin Hawley** (pp. 3-5; pp. 8-11; pp. 20-23); **Philip Webb** (p. 22); **Fraser Williamson** (cover; pp. 1-2; p. 7; pp. 12-13)
Photographed by **Rees Osborne Photography Ltd.**
Edited by **Frances Bacon**
Designed by **Kristie Rogers**

© 1997 Shortland Publications Inc.
All rights reserved.

09 08 07
11 10 9 8 7

Published in Australia and New Zealand by MIMOSA/McGraw-Hill,
8 Yarra Street, Hawthorn, Victoria 3122, Australia
Published in the United Kingdom by Kingscourt/McGraw-Hill,
Shoppenhangers Road, Maidenhead, Berkshire SL6 2QL

Printed in Hong Kong through Colorcraft Ltd
ISBN 10: 0-7901-1804-1
ISBN 13: 978-0-7901-1804-8